Be a RUGBY expert

Paul Mason

W

FRANKLIN WATTS

LONDON•SYDNEY

First published in 2015 by
Franklin Watts
338 Euston Road
London NW1 3BH

Franklin Watts Australia
Level 17/207 Kent Street
Sydney NSW 2000

HB ISBN 978 1 4451 4238 8
Library ebook ISBN 978 1 4451 4240 1

Dewey classification number: 796.333
A CIP catalogue record for this book is available from the British Library.

Editor: Julia Bird
Designer: D.R. ink

Photo acknowledgements: AFP/Getty Images: 5t, 25bl. albund/Shutterstock: 3. Archidea/Dreamstime: 11bl. Stephen Bisgrove/Alamy: 7br. Paolo Bona/Shutterstock: 4b, 7t, 7bl, 22t, 22c, 22b, 30t. Lionel Bonaventure/AFP/Getty Images: 14b. Gabriel Bouys/AFP/Getty Images: 8. Coloursport/Rex Features: 10br. Adrian Dennis/AFP/Getty Images: 20cr, 25c. Deymus HR/Shutterstock: 24. Alfredo Falcone/Dreamstime: 20b. Gallo Images/Getty Images: 13t. Getty Images: 4t, 14c, 23b. Graphitec/Dreamstime: 21cl. Grosremy/Dreamstime: 23cr. Mitch Gunn/Shutterstock: front cover. Help for Heroes: 15bl. Mark Herreid/Shutterstock: 5b. Mike Hewitt/Getty Images: 29b. Maurie Hill/Dreamstime: 20cl. Hilton123/Dreamstime: 21t. Tom Jenkins/Getty Images: 19b. Julicos/Dreamstime: 26cl. Mark Kolbe/Getty Images: 6t. Ross Land/Getty Images: 13b. Mark Leech/Getty Images: 2, 9t. Warren Little/Getty Images: 23t. Alex Livesey/Getty Images: 23cl. Maccers/Dreamstime: 21cr. Jordan Mansfield/Getty Images: 7c, 18, 21b, 30c. Maxirf/Dreamstime: 16b. Maxisport/Shutterstock: 15r, 30b. Maxisports/Dreamstime: 16t. Mingchai/Dreamstime: 17. The Photolibrary Wales/Alamy: 27c. Popperfoto/Getty Images: 6b, 10bl. Andrew Redington/Getty Images: 31t. Rixie/Dreamstime: 27t. David Rogers/Getty Images: 25br. Cameron Spencer/Getty Images: 19t. Mai Techapha/Shutterstock: 12. Patrick Valasseris/AFP/Getty Images: 11c. Phil Walter/Getty Images: front cover (Australia and New Zealand editions only).

Every attempt has been made to clear copyright. Should there be any inadvertent omission, please apply to the Publishers for rectification.

Franklin Watts is a division of Hachette Children's Books, an Hachette UK company.

www.hachette.co.uk

Printed in China

Every effort has been made by the Publishers to ensure that any websites included in this book are suitable for children, and that they contain no inappropriate or offensive material. However, because of the nature of the Internet, it is impossible to guarantee that the contents of these sites will not be altered. We strongly advise that Internet access is supervised by a responsible adult.

Contents

WHAT IS RUGBY?

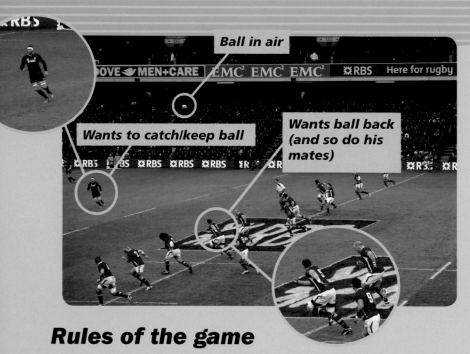

Ball in air

Wants to catch/keep ball

Wants ball back (and so do his mates)

Rugby is a reasonably simple game. To start, one team kicks the ball to the other. The team with the ball then has to move it to the far end of the pitch, and put it down. This is called 'scoring a try'.

Australian winger Drew Mitchell scores a flying try in the 2007 Rugby World Cup.

Rules of the game

Of course, rugby isn't QUITE as easy as it sounds. That's because:

a) The team without the ball is trying to stop you scoring. They do this by tackling: basically, dragging or throwing you to the ground. Then they try to grab the ball for themselves.

b) You're not allowed to throw the ball forward (which is the direction you need to go to score). Only sideways or backwards.

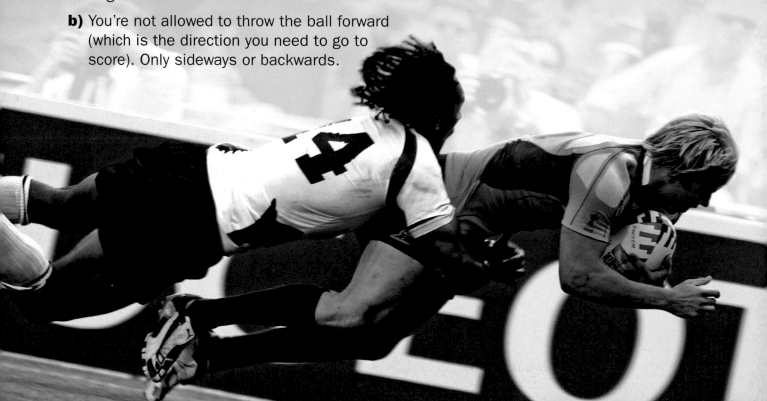

> # "Rugby is a hooligans' game, played by gentlemen."
>
> *Sir Winston Churchill, former British Prime Minister (1874–1965)*

A game for everyone

Whatever Winston Churchill might have said, rugby is played by males and females, old people and small children, and in over 100 different countries. It can be played by almost anyone, of any shape or size. Watch a top-level rugby match and you'll see that whether you are tall, short, heavy, light, fast or strong, there's a position somewhere on a rugby team that will suit you.

Types of rugby

There are lots of different types of rugby. There are versions for young players, practice games and games with seven players per team. This book is mainly about 15-a-side rugby union.

Rugby line-outs are always fiercely contested. Getting the ball quickly and cleanly makes fast attacks possible.

TECHNICALLY SPEAKING

Ways to get points in rugby union:

1) A try – worth **5 points**

2) Conversion of a try by kicking the ball between the posts – **2 points**

3) A penalty, kicking the ball between the posts after the other team has committed an offence – **3 points**

4) Drop goal, kicking the ball between the posts – **3 points**

POSITIONS: *FORWARDS*

A rugby team is divided into two groups, forwards and backs. The forwards' key job is to win the ball for the team. They also do a LOT of tackling. Forwards are therefore mostly large and strong. Sometimes – but not always – they are also fast.

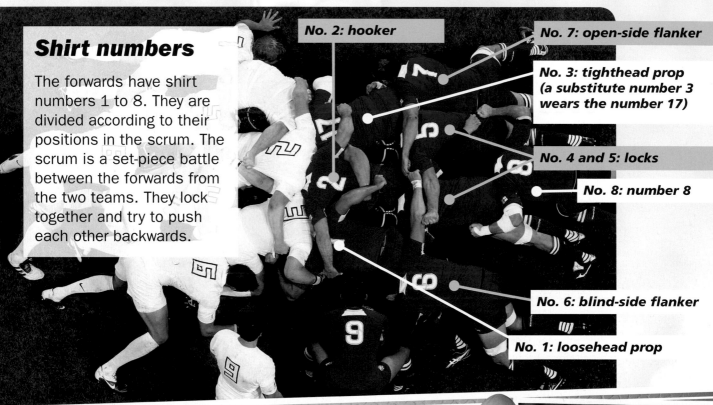

Shirt numbers

The forwards have shirt numbers 1 to 8. They are divided according to their positions in the scrum. The scrum is a set-piece battle between the forwards from the two teams. They lock together and try to push each other backwards.

No. 2: hooker

No. 7: open-side flanker

No. 3: tighthead prop (a substitute number 3 wears the number 17)

No. 4 and 5: locks

No. 8: number 8

No. 6: blind-side flanker

No. 1: loosehead prop

RUGBY LEGENDS

Name: JP du Randt

Team: South Africa

Position: Loosehead prop

Du Randt was known as Os (which means 'ox' in Afrikaans) because of his amazing strength. He first played for South Africa in 1994, won the World Cup in 1995, won it again in 2007, then finally retired from international rugby.

"There he goes – South Africa's rhino!"
Famous commentator Bill McLaren, describing Os du Randt in action.

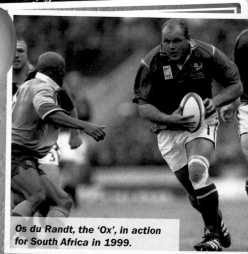

Os du Randt, the 'Ox', in action for South Africa in 1999.

Forward types

Each row of the scrum has a specific job to do. Because of this, they usually have particular physical characteristics.

Marcos Ayerza

Front-row players, such as Argentine loosehead prop Marcos Ayerza, have to hold up the scrum and push forward. They tend to be shorter and wider than other forwards, and very strong.

Second rows push the scrum forward, and are also used to jump into the air to catch the ball. They are usually the tallest players on the team. England lock Joanna McGilchrist is a second row player.

Joanna McGilchrist

Back row players have to be strong enough to push in the scrum, but also fast enough to join attacks quickly. New Zealand open-side flanker Richie McCaw is one of the most famous back row players.

Richie McCaw

TECHNICALLY SPEAKING
Cauliflower ear

Rugby forwards often have 'cauliflower' ears. This is just as unpleasant as it sounds. Their ears get bashed or squashed, and puff up with blood. The only treatments are: a) drain the blood or b) wear a head-guard so you don't get cauliflower ear in the first place.

POSITIONS: BACKS

In a rugby team, if you're not a forward, you're a back. (Two of the backs are often called 'half-backs' – see page 9.) There are seven backs, wearing numbers 9 to 15. Their key job is to move the ball forward by running with it in their hands or by kicking it.

Run away

Backs tend to be fast-moving, agile players with good ball-handling skills. Their speed helps them escape the clutches of any forwards waiting to tackle them. (This is a good thing, assuming you don't like being smashed to the ground and squashed.) There are exceptions to the smaller/faster rule of course – see the panel on Jonah Lomu for a particularly large one.

Bryan Habana of South Africa is a famous back. Here he escapes a last-ditch attempt at a tap tackle by Danie Dames of Namibia.

RUGBY LEGENDS

Name: Jonah Lomu
Team: New Zealand
Position: Winger

Lomu was enormous (1.96 m tall and 120 kg) at the height of his career, but could run 100 metres in 10.89 seconds. He was almost unstoppable, and often just ran over opponents who tried to tackle him.

"Remember that rugby is a team game: all 14 of you make sure you pass the ball to Jonah."

Fax to the New Zealand team before the 1995 World Cup semi-final. Lomu went on to score four tries, leading the All Blacks to the final (which they lost).

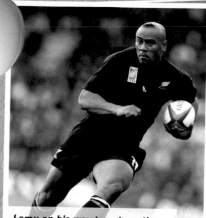

Lomu on his way to yet another try for the All Blacks.

Shirt numbers

You can tell from a back's shirt number roughly where they will be positioned on the pitch:

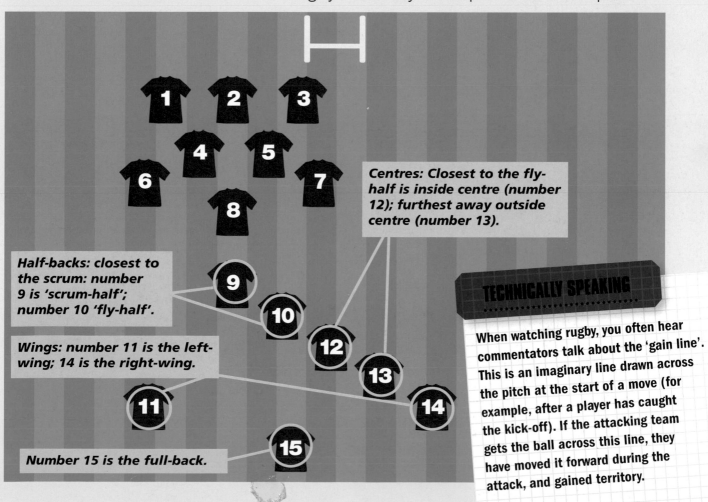

Centres: Closest to the fly-half is inside centre (number 12); furthest away outside centre (number 13).

Half-backs: closest to the scrum: number 9 is 'scrum-half'; number 10 'fly-half'.

Wings: number 11 is the left-wing; 14 is the right-wing.

Number 15 is the full-back.

TECHNICALLY SPEAKING

When watching rugby, you often hear commentators talk about the 'gain line'. This is an imaginary line drawn across the pitch at the start of a move (for example, after a player has caught the kick-off). If the attacking team gets the ball across this line, they have moved it forward during the attack, and gained territory.

THE GREATEST TRY EVER SCORED

Of all the ways to score points in rugby, a try is the most spectacular. Tries are scored in all kinds of ways, from a lone player racing the length of the pitch to a mob of forwards bundling the ball over the line. Amazingly though, many rugby experts agree on which was the Greatest Try Ever.

Barbarian brilliance

In 1973 New Zealand arrived at Cardiff Arms Park in Wales to play an international invitational team called the Barbarians. Few people gave the 'Baa-Baas' much chance. New Zealand had already beaten Wales, Scotland and England. But then the Baa-Baas scored a try that has become known as the best ever.

The attack started close to the Barbarian line, with some amazing sidesteps from the fly-half, Phil Bennett. Five passes – including an amazing fingertip catch by the forward Derek Quinnell – and a lot of swerving running later, Barbarian scrum-half Gareth Edwards scored. New Zealand eventually lost the match 23–11.

Name: Gareth Edwards

Team: Wales

Position: Scrum-half

Edwards was the youngest Wales captain ever. He was just 20 when he led his country for the first time, in 1968. Famous as the scorer of rugby's unofficial Best Try Ever Scored (see right).

The Barbarians, wearing hooped shirts, attack in the build-up to the Greatest Try Ever Scored. The player who finally crossed New Zealand's line with the ball, Gareth Edwards, is second from the right.

More top tries

These three tries are also among the best ever scored. Ask an adult to help you find videos of all of these tries on the Internet.

The 'Try From the End of the World', France against New Zealand, 1994

At some points during the build-up it seems every French player must have touched the ball, before full-back Jean-Luc Sadourny broke away to score a fantastic try.

2

Takudzwa Ngyenya of USA against South Africa, 2007

Winger Ngyenya (below) goes round the outside of Bryan Habana, then known as 'the fastest player in the world', as if Habana is jogging.

3

Rupeni Caucaunibuca of Fiji against France, 2003

The sheer speed of 'Caucau' makes it look as though everyone else is stuck in slow motion, or running through mud.

TECHNICALLY SPEAKING

Why is a try called a try? It is because back in the early days of rugby, you didn't get any points for touching the ball down at the end of the pitch. All you got was the chance to try and score a goal, by kicking the ball between the posts. Touching the ball down became known as winning a 'try'.

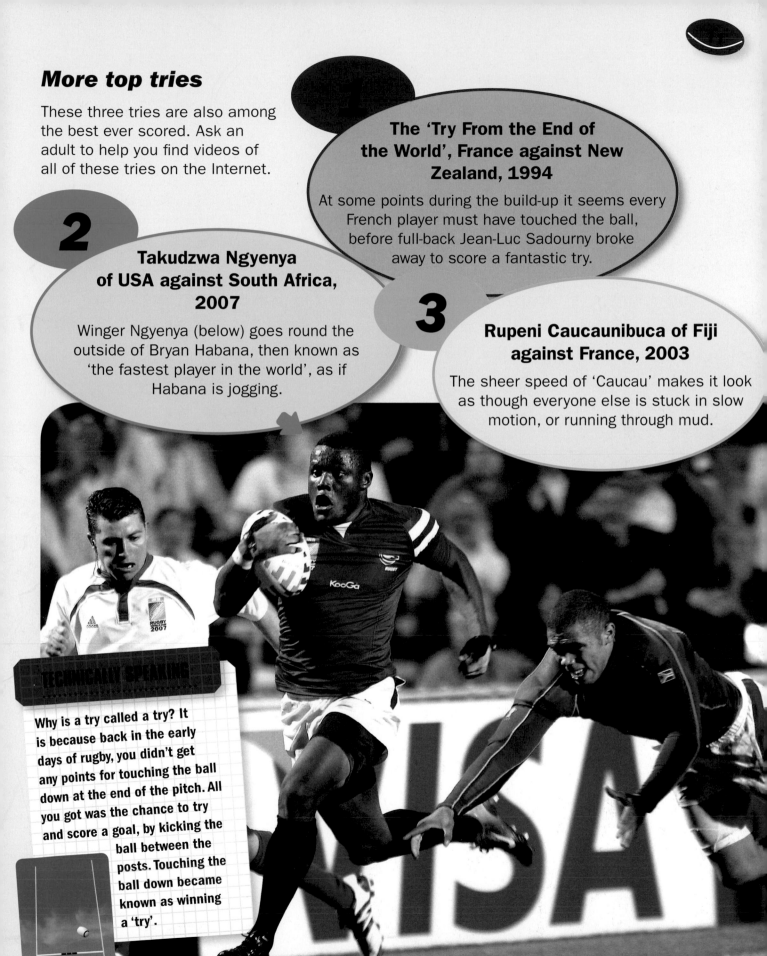

BIG HITS: THE ART OF TACKLING

Defenders can tackle any opposition attacker who has the ball. They aim to a) stop the attacker moving forward, b) stop them passing or kicking the ball away and c) either knock the ball loose or get it back for their own team.

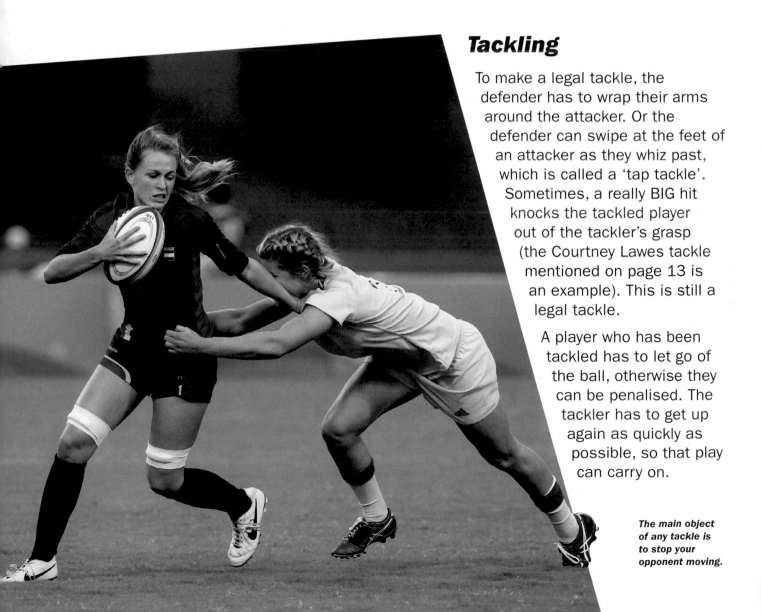

Tackling

To make a legal tackle, the defender has to wrap their arms around the attacker. Or the defender can swipe at the feet of an attacker as they whiz past, which is called a 'tap tackle'. Sometimes, a really BIG hit knocks the tackled player out of the tackler's grasp (the Courtney Lawes tackle mentioned on page 13 is an example). This is still a legal tackle.

A player who has been tackled has to let go of the ball, otherwise they can be penalised. The tackler has to get up again as quickly as possible, so that play can carry on.

The main object of any tackle is to stop your opponent moving.

Rugby's biggest hitters

Some players are particularly excellent at knocking over opponents. Searching out videos of big hits by these five is always worthwhile:

- **Jerry 'The Hitman' Collins**, New Zealand
- **Thierry Dusautoir**, France
- **Courtney Lawes**, England (look for 'tackle on Nicky Robinson')
- **Brian 'the Chiropractor'* Lima**, Samoa (look for 'tackle on Derrick Hougaard')
  *An ACTUAL chiropractor treats problems with people's bones, rather than creating them.
- **Bismarck du Plessis**, South Africa

Thierry Dusautoir (centre) and Cedric Heymans of France (right), determined to stop South Africa's Adrian Jacobs in his tracks.

TECHNICALLY SPEAKING

Some tackles just aren't allowed, because they are dangerous. The referee can award a penalty kick to the opposition, a yellow card and time in the sin bin, or a red card and being sent off the pitch if they see any of these:

- **High tackle:** tackling a player above the shoulders
- **Tip tackle:** picking up a tackled player and dumping them on their head or back
- **Barging** into a player
- **Tackling** a player in the air.

Irish back Jamie Heaslip is shown a red card during an international match.

When does a tackle become a ruck?

Once a tackled player has let go of the ball, anyone can pick it up as long as they are on their feet. Usually, players from BOTH teams try to get hold of it, and a pushing match called a ruck forms. Each team tries to shove the opposition away from the ball so that they can get at it.

The difference between a ruck and a maul

If the player has been grabbed by the opposition but NOT hit the ground before the pushing match between the two teams gets going, it's called a maul instead of a ruck.

SCRUMS AND LINE-OUTS

Sometimes, the game stops. Actually, in rugby it stops quite often. Someone drops the ball, kicks it off the pitch or puts their foot on the touchline by accident while holding it.

Starting again

When the game stops like this, the referee decides whose fault it was and gives the ball to the other team. The restart is usually a contest between the teams. The two key ways of restarting the game are the scrum and the line-out.

Scrums

Scrums are normally used to restart the game if the action has stopped without the ball going off the pitch. The scrum is a pushing contest between the two packs of forwards. The first few scrums of the match can be a good indicator of which team will win. If one pack is much stronger than the other, their team has the advantage.

Scrums can be a good opportunity to score a try if they are held near the try line. Players force the ball over the try line using the power and weight of the pack.

"If anyone says the scrum doesn't matter, try telling that to the crowd here."

Commentator Brian Moore, a former England hooker, talks about England's demolition of Ireland's scrum in 2012.

Knock-ons

Knocking the ball forward (except by kicking it) is called a 'knock-on'. The game stops and is restarted with a scrum. The other team gets to put the ball into the scrum.

Line-outs

When the ball goes out of play over the touchline, the game usually restarts with a line-out. Up to seven forwards from each team form a line, starting five metres from the sideline. Hookers do not join the lines. The hooker from the attacking team throws the ball from the touchline straight between the two lines. The aim is for a teammate to jump in the air and catch it. The defending team can also try to get the ball. Like the scrum a dominant line-out for one team can change the course of the match.

Tackling the jumper at a line-out is not allowed. Getting in their way, making the ball harder to catch, is allowed – as you can see here.

RUGBY UNION LEGENDS

Name: Martin Johnson

Team: England

Position: Lock

Johnson was a line-out expert, famous for taking the ball on the opposition's throw-in. He captained England through their best winning streak. From 2002–03 England was almost unbeatable, and in 2003 the team won the Rugby World Cup for the first time.

BIG COMPETITIONS

Wherever you are in the world, you probably won't be far from a game of rugby. The sport is played in over 100 countries, and on every continent except Antarctica. But where will you find the really TOP competitions each year?

Southern hemisphere

At a club level, the biggest contest is Super Rugby. This is played between 15 teams from Australia, New Zealand and South Africa. Internationally, every year teams from these three countries, plus Argentina, play for the Rugby Championship.

Northern hemisphere

In the northern hemisphere, the biggest annual club competition is the Champions Cup. This features the top 20 teams in Europe. French clubs won the old version, the Heineken Cup, seven times and English and Irish clubs six times each, before it was renamed in 2014.

The biggest international competition is the Six Nations, which is played every year between England, France, Ireland, Italy, Scotland and Wales. This was originally the Five Nations, but then Italy joined in 2000.

A Rugby Sevens match underway in Hong Kong, which holds an international Sevens competition every year.

Test matches

The northern and southern hemispheres collide in a series of international test matches. In November and December, teams from the southern hemisphere visit Europe to play international matches. During June and July, European countries send their teams south, to play in Argentina, Australia, South Africa or New Zealand.

Olympic rugby

The USA is a good rugby side, but not one of the top teams in the world. So it might be a surprise to discover that they are the reigning 15-a-side Olympic rugby champions. This odd fact is because rugby was last part of the Olympics in 1924, when the USA won the title by defeating the only other team to enter, France. Rugby returns to the list of Olympic sports in Brazil in 2016, when the Sevens version of the game is included.

TECHNICALLY SPEAKING

SEVENS

Sevens is a form of rugby played with just seven players per team (which is how it got the name...). Each match lasts just 14 minutes (7 per half), so the action is fast and furious. There are fewer stoppages than in 15-a-side, and the play is easier to understand. Sevens has its own world series, which attracts big audiences.

THE RUGBY WORLD CUP

Rugby's top competition is the World Cup. The World Cup is like the Olympics: it only comes along every four years. There are versions for men and women. By 2011, New Zealand, Australia and South Africa had each won the men's version twice, and England once.

Blast from the past (literally)

The first game of every Rugby World Cup tournament is started with a blast from the same whistle. The whistle was first used in 1905 to start a match between England and New Zealand. It was also used during the final rugby match at the 1924 Paris Olympics.

How do you win the World Cup?

It's easy: you just have to keep winning matches. At the start of the contest the teams are in groups or 'pools'. The teams in each pool play one another, and the two with the most points then go through to the knockout stages. These get their name from the fact that if you lose a match, you're knocked out of the tournament. If you win instead, and keep winning, you eventually make it to the final. Win that, and you've won the World Cup.

England's Emily Scarratt on the rampage in the final of the 2014 women's Rugby World Cup.

New Zealand celebrate victory at the 2011 Rugby World Cup.

TECHNICALLY SPEAKING

TWO POINTS A MINUTE
The Rugby World Cup game with the highest number of points scored took place in 1995. New Zealand beat Japan 145 points to 17, so in 80 minutes of play there were 162 points scored. That's 2.025 points a minute!

RUGBY WORLD CUP 2011
CHAMPIONS

ALL BLACKS

RUGBY LEGENDS

Name: Jonny Wilkinson

Team: England

Position: Fly-half

An England player at just 18, Wilkinson had set a series of records by the time he retired in 2014:

- Winner of three Six Nations titles and a World Cup with England
- Highest points scorer in international rugby (later overtaken by Dan Carter, see page 20)
- Winner of the European club contest three times with the French side Toulon

Perhaps Jonny's biggest achievement is to be the only English player EVER to be as popular in France as in England.

"I only get the points because I have teammates who do the work."
Jonny Wilkinson in typical modest form.

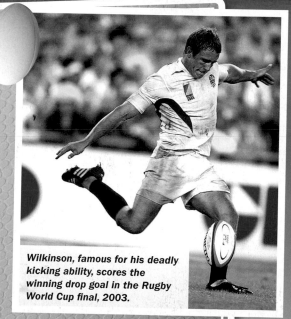

Wilkinson, famous for his deadly kicking ability, scores the winning drop goal in the Rugby World Cup final, 2003.

THE WORLD'S TOP PLAYERS

Rugby is a team game. Often the players you don't notice, who hardly get mentioned by the commentators, are doing a crucial job for their side. But rugby has superstars too, players so skilful that they can turn a match on their own. So, who are the names to watch out for at the next big competition?

Sergio Parisse
Team: Italy
Position: Number 8

Parisse is a rare thing: an Italian player good enough to play for top teams such as France or Australia. Many people think that Parisse could be the world's best Number 8.

Richie McCaw
Team: New Zealand
Position: Flanker

Broke into the All Black back row at 20, when he won Man of the Match in his first game, and captain from 2006. McCaw is famous for his skill at getting hold of the ball during a ruck. Regularly voted the world's best player.

Dan Carter
Team: New Zealand
Position: Fly-half

Carter is arguably rugby's greatest ever fly-half. He has certainly scored more international points than any other, breaking Jonny Wilkinson's record of 1,246 points in 2011.

Victor Matfield

Team: South Africa
Position: Lock

Matfield has an amazing ability to work out which opposition jumper will get the ball in a line-out. South Africa also has a young lock called Eben Etzebeth who seems likely to be as good as Matfield – if not better.

Bryan Habana

Team: South Africa
Position: Wing

Famed as the world's fastest player, Habana was one of the stars of South Africa's victory at the 2007 World Cup. He may have lost a little speed since then – but he's still quicker than 99 per cent of the world's top players.

Emily Scarratt

Team: England
Position: Centre/full-back

Scarratt hit the headlines when England won the World Cup in 2014, scoring a try and kicking 11 points. At just 24, she had already been an international for six years, and has been compared to greats of the game such as Jonny Wilkinson (see page 19).

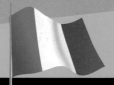

Paul O'Connell

Team: Ireland
Position: Lock

To opponents, O'Connell is a glowering, intimidating presence on the pitch. His inspirational attitude and playing skills have seen him captain both Ireland and the British and Irish Lions invitational team.

GREAT TEAMS

Some teams always stand a chance of winning, even when they are not playing well. Take England at the 2007 World Cup. Playing poorly, and thumped 36–0 by South Africa in their opening game, they still managed to reach the final. (Where they lost to South Africa again, 15–6.)

Beware...

So, which teams should their opponents always watch out for?

1. NEW ZEALAND

Ranked the world's number one rugby team every year since 2004, New Zealand is the team no one wants to see in their group at a big tournament.

New Zealand performs the intimidating haka *at the start of each match.*

2. SOUTH AFRICA

South Africa takes pride in its large, powerful forwards (as well as its large, powerful backs). Opponents who underestimate the physical force of the South African attack tend to get blown away. Uruguay found this to its cost in 2005, when the Springboks won 134–3.

3. AUSTRALIA

In recent years, Australia has rarely put together a strong enough forward pack to overpower its opponents. Australia's backs, though, are able to launch surprise attacks from anywhere on the pitch.

Phil Waugh of Australia scrambles away a pass.

4. ENGLAND

England's great strength is its awesome forward pack. In a game with lots of tactical kicking, scrums, line-outs, rucks and mauls, most other teams find England extremely hard to beat.

5. FRANCE

France is the king of upsetting big tournament favourites. Most memorably, France defeated New Zealand (the hot favourite) 20–18 in the quarter final of the 2007 World Cup.

6. WALES

When the Welsh team plays well, it is a threat to any team. England often finds them a stumbling block – they came close to being beaten by Wales in the 2003 World Cup, which England eventually won.

RUGBY LEGENDS

Name: David Campese

Team: Australia

Position: Wing/full-back

Campese or 'Campo' is an all-time Australian great. He scored an amazing 64 tries in 101 international matches, and when he retired in 1996 had played more games for his country than any other player. Campo won the Rugby World Cup in 1991, giving one of the performances of his career.

David Campese shows off his distinctive high-stepping run.

What's in a name?

International rugby teams often have a nickname as well known as their ACTUAL name:

Actual name	Nickname
Australia	Wallabies
Barbarians	Baa-baas
British and Irish Lions	Lions
France	Les Bleus
Italy	The Azzurri
Japan	Brave Blossoms
New Zealand (men's)	All Blacks
New Zealand (women's)	Black Ferns
Romania	Oaks
South Africa	Springboks
Argentina	Pumas
USA	Eagles
Wales	Dragons/Red Dragons

2015 – THE WORLD CUP COMES TO ENGLAND

In 2015, the great rugby teams come together when England hosts the eighth Rugby World Cup. England won the trophy in 2003, and was in the final in 1991 and 2007. Playing on home soil isn't necessarily an advantage, though. At the seven previous World Cups, only South Africa and New Zealand triumphed at home.

Many matches

For anyone who doesn't like rugby, it might be a good idea to take a six-week holiday starting 18 September 2015. That's when the Rugby World Cup kicks off, with England v Fiji at the Millennium Stadium, Cardiff (although England are the official hosts of the tournament, some matches are being played in Wales). By the time the World Cup finishes with the final at Twickenham on 31 October, 20 teams will have played 48 matches between them. The games will have been watched live by well over two million people, and on TV by tens of millions more.

The Millennium Stadium, Cardiff – the only non-English stadium to be used in the 2015 World Cup.

TECHNICALLY SPEAKING

Every big international contest has a 'Group of Death' – one that contains several top teams, which will be especially hard to win. At the 2015 World Cup, the Group of Death was generally agreed to be Pool A, featuring England, Australia, Wales, Fiji and Uruguay.

Live action

The matches of the 2015 World Cup are to be played all around the country:

MIDLANDS
*Villa Park, Birmingham;
The King Power Stadium,
Leicester; Stadium mk,
Milton Keynes*

THE WEST
*Sandy Park, Exeter;
Kingsholm, Gloucester;
Millennium Stadium, Cardiff*

NORTHERN ENGLAND
*St James's Park, Newcastle; The
Etihad Stadium, Manchester;
Elland Road, Leeds*

**LONDON AND SOUTH-
EAST ENGLAND**
*Twickenham, Wembley
and Olympic Stadium,
London; Brighton
Community Stadium*

Three to watch out for

The World Cup always features the best players, and there is a selection of these on pages 20–21. Here, though, are just three of the young players who could become the stars of tomorrow:

Manu Tuilagi, centre, England

Nailed on for the England team since 2011, Tuilagi combines speed, handling skills, size and aggressive tackling.

Julian Savea, wing, New Zealand

An All Black at 19 years old, Savea is fast, strong and big (1.93 metres tall and 108 kg), and has been compared to the great Jonah Lomu (see page 9).

Gael Ficou, centre, France

First played for France in 2013 at the age of 18, and has been tipped as one of the world's best centres ever since. Blends tremendous speed with amazing balance, and is tough to tackle as a result.

RUGBY ODDITIES

Rugby throws up some odd facts. These are a bit like the bounce of its odd-shaped ball: unpredictable, and sometimes surprising. Here are a few rugby oddities – starting, in fact, with two about the rugby ball itself:

FACT 1: RUGBY BALLS WEREN'T ALWAYS OVAL

In fact, they started off being round – or at least, as close to round as possible. Because they were stitched from pig's bladders, they tended to end up plum-shaped. This made the game much more fun, and when perfect round balls became available, the authorities decided to stick with oval ones.

2: RUGBY BALLS CAN BE DANGEROUS

A man named Richard Lindon made the first rugby balls for Rugby School from pigs' bladders. He got Mrs Lindon to blow the balls up for him. She is said to have died as a result of breathing in air from diseased bladders.

3: SCOTLAND WON THE FIRST INTERNATIONAL MATCH

The first international was between Scotland and England in 1871. Using rugby's original scoring system (see page 11), Scotland won 1–0. Scotland scored two tries and one conversion; England got a try, but failed to convert.

4: THE LONGEST GAME LASTED A DAY (AND A NIGHT)

In 2011, Congleton Rugby Union Football Club in Cheshire in the UK created two teams, the Mali Lions and the Congleton RUFC Bears, with the aim of setting a new world record for the longest rugby match ever played. The match lasted a record-busting 24 hours, 30 minutes and 6 seconds. The Lions won 894–715.

5: SPEEDIEST FLIGHT

The fastest throw of a rugby ball was 77.25 km/h by Joe Simpson (left), a professional rugby player for London Wasps, in 2011.

6: TIME FOR A SONG

Nowadays, it is traditional for the national anthems to be sung before major international contests. The first time this happened was before a rugby game. On 16 November 1905, after New Zealand danced its traditional *haka* dance before the match, Wales responded by starting to sing the Welsh national anthem, *Hen Wlad Fy Nhadau*. The crowd picked up on this and joined in.

" Crazy quotes

If you've just spent 80 minutes running around a rugby field, your thoughts might be a bit scrambled – which probably explains some of these quotes from players:

"Nobody in rugby should be called a genius. A genius is a guy like Norman Einstein."

New Zealand flanker Jono Gibbes

"Colin has done a bit of mental arithmetic with a calculator."

All Black centre Ma'a Nonu

"I never comment on referees, and I'm not going to break the habit of a lifetime for that prat."

Australia coach Ewan McKenzie manages to get his point across anyway.

"I've never had major knee surgery on any other part of my body."

Jerry 'The Hitman' Collins of New Zealand

COMMENTATOR-SPEAK DECIPHERED

If you watch rugby on TV – which is how most people see big contests such as the World Cup – you will probably be listening to commentators. They use words that even experienced rugby watchers stumble over. This fast guide will help decipher what you're hearing:

Advantage
If a team commits an offence, the referee can 'play advantage'. They let play continue if stopping it would cause the non-offending team to lose a good position. The referee waits to see what happens, then blows the whistle if necessary later

Box kick
A kick from behind a scrum, ruck or maul, usually by the scrum-half, which goes high into the air but does not travel very far

Charge down
Blocking a kick, by running towards the kicker and stopping the ball after it has been kicked

Grubber kick
A low kick that bounces along the ground, always unpredictably due to the oval shape of a rugby ball

Hospital pass
A pass that leads to the receiving player being smashed down in an inevitable tackle

Knock-on
When a player knocks the ball forward in any way other than kicking it, it is known as a knock-on. The game usually restarts with a scrum: the other team gets to put the ball in

Mark
Place where play will restart after a stoppage. Players can also call for a 'mark' when they catch the ball in their own 22 or in-goal area. All their teammates get behind them, and the catcher can then kick the ball back to the opposition

Obstruction — Getting in the way of an opponent who does not have the ball, as a way of blocking them from taking part in the action

Offside — There are offside rules for open play, rucks, scrums, etc. Basically, a player is offside if he or she is too far forward to legally play the ball

Penalty — Punishment for breaking the rules, which results in a kick at goal for the non-offending team. If the kick goes over, they get 3 points

Red card — Shown by the referee as a punishment, to send a player off the pitch for the rest of the game

Sin bin — An area where a player who has received a yellow card sits out of the game for 10 minutes

Touch — The sides of the pitch (which includes the lines painted to mark the sides)

Turnover — When one side wins possession of the ball from the other

Twenty-two — Line across the pitch 22 metres from the in-goal area

Yellow card — Shown by the referee as a punishment, to send a player off the pitch to the sin bin for the next 10 minutes of playing time

Curse of the commentators

For people who are paid to speak clearly, commentators sometimes say surprising things. Here are three top trip-ups:

"Strangely, in slow-motion replay, the ball seemed to hang in the air for even longer."
All Black turned commentator Murray Mexted

"That kick was absolutely unique. Except for the one before it, which was identical."
Tony Brown, coach of Otago RFU, New Zealand

"I think you enjoy the game more if you don't know the rules. Anyway, you're on the same wavelength as the referees."
Jonathan Davies, former Wales player

Welsh rugby legend, now BBC commentator, Jonathan Davies

RUGBY BRAIN-ACHE:
TEST YOURSELF

1 What is a half-back?

a) a very short player
b) a player who stands close to the scrum, and wears number 9 or 10 on their shirt
c) a technique for doubling back on the opposition

2 Who are the current Olympic champions at rugby?

a) New Zealand, probably: they've won everything else
b) The USA
c) No one: rugby isn't even in the Olympics until Sevens becomes part of it in 2016

3 Which team has won the Rugby World Cup more times than any other?

a) New Zealand, they're always the favourites
b) No one: three teams have won it twice each
c) Brazil

4 If someone does a 'grubber kick', are they:

a) Kicking the ball along the ground so that it bounces unpredictably
b) Kicking the ball through mud to make it dirty
c) Kicking an opponent because he or she has a grubby shirt, and it reflects badly on everyone

5 Which team is known as the Baa-baas?

a) Wales, because everyone knows there are loads of sheep in Wales
b) France, because of their funny accents
c) The Barbarians

How many did you get right?

1–2 Cauliflower ear? More like brain!
3–4 You're no Jonah Lomu, but not a bad performance.
5 Congratulations – you're a rugby expert!

GETTING INTO RUGBY

One of the best things about rugby is that you do not have to be a hulking, 1.9-metre giant to play. There are versions of the sport for almost everyone. Children usually start with tag rugby, where instead of tackling someone you grab a coloured tag from the side of their clothing. Touch rugby is also popular, where touching someone replaces tackling them; this is played by adults, as well as kids.

The best way to get into rugby is either through school or a local club. If you want to find your local club, the easiest way is through the national governing body.

England: The Rugby Football Union (www.englandrugby.com)

Ireland: Irish Rugby (www.irishrugby.ie)

Scotland: Scottish Rugby (www.scottishrugby.org)

Wales: The Welsh Rugby Union (www.wru.co.uk)

Australia: The Australian Rugby Union (www.rugby.com.au)

New Zealand: New Zealand Rugby (www.nzrugby.co.nz)

Finding out more

The websites of the governing bodies are a good place to find out more about rugby, especially some of the rules and leading international players. You can also find out dates of matches and similar details.

For information about the 2015 Rugby World Cup, the websites www.rugbyworldcup.com (for the men's contest) and www.rwcwomens.com are good starting places.

There are also lots of good books on rugby. These are particularly worth looking out:

Rugby Union (A&C Black, 2006)
Good, clear explanations of the different forms of rugby and the rules, endorsed by the Rugby Football Union.

Skills: Tackling, Contact, Teamwork, Tactics and *Skills: Passing, Catching, Kicking* Simon Jones (A&C Black, 2009)
Each of these books teaches young players (and their coaches) ways of building up rugby skills in a fun, safe way.

Know Your Sport: Rugby Clive Gifford (Franklin Watts, 2012)
A hands-on introduction to the rules, techniques and skills of rugby, backed up by step-by-step photos and biographies of top players.

Index